Helping Children
with Feelings

# Helping Children who Yearn for Someone they Love

The Frog
who Longed
for the Moon
to Smile

## A Guidebook

Margot Sunderland

Illustrated by

Nicky Armstrong

Speechmark

www.speechmark.net

**Note on the Text**
For the sake of clarity alone, throughout the text the child has been referred to as 'he' and the parent as 'she'.

Unless otherwise stated, for clarity alone, where 'mummy', 'mother' or 'mother figure' is used, this refers to either parent or other primary caretaker.

**Confidentiality**
Where appropriate, full permission has been granted by adults, or children and their parents, to use clinical material. Other illustrations comprise synthesised and disguised examples to ensure anonymity.

Published by
**Speechmark Publishing Ltd**
2$^{nd}$ Floor, 5 Thomas More Square, London E1W 1YW, UK
**www.speechmark.net**

First published 2000
Reprinted 2003, 2009, 2015

002-5067/Printed in the United Kingdom/1010

**British Library Cataloguing in Publication Data**
Sunderland, Margot
   The frog who longed for the moon to smile : helping children who yearn for someone they love
   Guidebook. – (Stories for Troubled Children)
   1. Storytelling – Therapeutic use 2. Child psychology 3. Learning, Psychology of
   I. Title II. Armstrong, Nicky
   615.8'516

ISBN 978 0 86388 456 6

# Contents

# ABOUT THE AUTHOR

MARGOT SUNDERLAND is Founding Director of the Centre for Child Mental Health, London. She is also Head of the Children and Young People Section of The United Kingdom Association for Therapeutic Counselling. In addition, she formed the research project, 'Helping Where it Hurts' which offers free therapy and counselling to troubled children in several primary schools in North London. She is a registered Integrative Arts Psychotherapist and registered Child Therapeutic Counsellor, Supervisor and Trainer.

Margot is also Principal of The Institute for Arts in Therapy and Education – a fully accredited Higher Education College running a Diploma course in Child Therapy and Masters Degree courses in Arts Psychotherapy and Arts in Education and Therapy.

Margot is a published poet and author of two non-fiction books – one on *Dance* (Routledge Theatre Arts, New York and J Garnet Miller, England) and the other called *Draw on Your Emotions* (Speechmark Publishing, Bicester and Erickson, Italy).

# ABOUT THE ILLUSTRATOR

NICKY ARMSTRONG holds an MA from The Slade School of Fine Art and a BA Hons in Theatre Design from the University of Central England. She is currently teacher of trompe l'œil at The Hampstead School of Decorative Arts, London. She has achieved major commissions nationally and internationally in mural work and fine art.

# ACKNOWLEDGEMENTS

A special acknowledgement to Mattan Lederman who, at age seven, drew an entire set of pictures for all of the five stories in the pack. Several of his ideas and designs were then adopted by the illustrator.

I would like to thank Katherine Pierpont, Charlotte Emmett and Ruth Bonner for all their superb skill and rigour in the editing process, and for making the long writing journey such a pleasurable one.

I would also like to thank all the children, trainees and supervisees with whom I have worked, whose poetry, images and courage have greatly enriched both my work and my life.

# ABOUT THIS GUIDEBOOK

If a child is going to benefit from the full therapeutic potential of *The Frog who Longed for the Moon to Smile*, this accompanying guidebook will be a vital resource. We strongly advise that you read it before reading the story itself to the child. By doing so, you will come to the child from a far more informed position, and so you will be able to offer him a far richer, and more empathic, response.

This guidebook details the common psychological origins and most relevant psychotherapeutic theories for the problems and issues addressed in the story. If you read it before reading the story to the child, it will prevent your coming to the child from an ignorant or closed viewpoint about why he is troubled. For example, 'I'm sure that Johnny's school work has gone downhill because he is missing his Daddy, who moved out a few months ago' may be an accurate or inaccurate hypothesis. There may be many other reasons for Johnny's problems with his school work, which have not been considered. The problem may well be complex, as so many psychological problems are. Coming from a closed or too narrow viewpoint all too often means that the helping adult is in danger of projecting on to the child *their own* feelings and views about the world.

Very few parents are consciously cruel. When something goes wrong in the parenting of a child, it is often to do with the parent *not knowing* about some vital aspect of child psychology or child development, or a lack in the way the parent was brought up themselves. There is still a tragic gap between what is known about effective parenting in child psychology, psychotherapy and scientific research, and how much of this is communicated to parents via parenting books or through television and the press. So this guidebook is not about blaming parents. Rather, the aim is to support. More generally, the aim is to heighten the awareness of *anyone* looking after children about how things can go wrong (usually despite the best intentions), and about how to help them go right in the first place, or to get mended if they do go wrong.

This guidebook includes what children themselves have said about what it is like trying to cope with the problems and issues addressed in the story, and describes the stories they have enacted through their play. It includes a section that offers suggestions and ideas for things to say and do after you have read *The Frog who Longed for the Moon to Smile* to the child. The suggestions and ideas are specifically designed to help a child to think about, express and further digest his feelings about the particular problems and issues addressed in the story. Some of the exercises are also designed to inspire children to speak more about what they are feeling through *their own* spontaneous story-making.

Everyday language is not the natural language for children to use to speak about what they feel. But, with an adult they trust, they can usually show or enact, draw or play out their feelings very well indeed. Therefore many of the exercises offered in this guidebook will support the child in creative, imaginative and playful ways of expressing himself. Also, so that you avoid asking too many questions, interrogating the child about their feeling life (to which children do not respond at all well), some of the exercises simply require the child to tick a box, 'show me', or pick a word or an image from a selection.

# INTRODUCTION

## What the story is about

Frog is very much in love with the moon, because once the moon smiled at him. Now he spends all his time gazing at her and dreaming about her. He waits and waits for her to smile at him again. But one day, a wise and friendly crow helps Frog to see how he is wasting away his life like this. And so, eventually, Frog dares to turn away from the moon. When he does, he feels a terrible emptiness and terrible aloneness, but when, in time, he looks around him, he is lit up by everything he sees. He cries as he realises how, all the time he has been facing the 'place of giving-very-little', and how he has had his back to the 'place of plenty'.

## The main psychological messages in this story

☆ When you are facing the gates of hell, you have your back to the gates of heaven.

☆ While you give all your attention, all your love, and all your loyalty to an emotionally bleak relationship, you are turning your back on the possibility of enjoying an emotionally nourishing one.

☆ The more you cling to someone, the less likely it is that you will feel held by them.

☆ By yearning for someone who *cannot* love you, you are depriving yourself of a relationship with someone who *can*.

☆ Metaphorically speaking, if someone wants to come and play in your garden, that's great. If they don't, that's fine too. Find someone who does.

☆ It is a pointless waste of time trying to persuade someone who does not love you that they do.

☆ Just because the moon/parent/friend does not smile at you, it does not mean that there is anything wrong with you. It is just that some people cannot love and some people dare not let themselves love.

☆ There can be life after losing too much – and not just life, but very rich life.

✬ If you stop trying to get someone who cannot love you to love you, there can be a very dark time, with no sight of land, and then, after a time, you can be washed up on a beautiful island. But in the dark times, it is possible to forget that there are any islands at all.

✬ All the beauty and loveliness in the world is never in just one person, although to a love-addicted adult or child, it can feel like it is.

✬ You may be focusing on something so unreachable that you miss something wonderful which is right in front of you.

✬ There is always something brighter around the corner which you cannot see in a dark time.

✬ Do not mistake rarities for pearls.

## Who the story is for

So much has been written about adult pain in love. So little is said about a child's pain in love. The story is for children who are suffering in one or more ways:

✬ Children who are missing someone too much.

✬ Children who suffer from separation anxiety.

✬ Children for whom their absent parent has become an obsession.

✬ Children who yearn because they feel they cannot light up the person they love.

✬ Children who yearn for a parent who seems unreachable, although she is right there.

✬ Children who yearn for a parent who is loving one minute and indifferent, cold or abusive the next.

✬ Children who yearn because they have been taken into care, fostered or adopted.

✬ Children who yearn for a parent who has died.

# WHAT LIFE IS LIKE FOR CHILDREN WHO YEARN

I cannot find me because I don't know where you are. (Sally, aged nine, to her depressed mother)

The story of Frog can be read to children who are missing someone so badly that they cannot be fully with anything that is happening to them in the present. In fact, the intensity of their missing may be adversely affecting their school work. Some just stare out of the window, like Ben, aged six, whose Daddy had moved out because of the divorce; or like Sally, aged eight, who had been sent to boarding school. Other younger children are very much like Frog in that, on being left in the nursery, they keep their eyes glued to the door through which Mummy left. Others try to keep her alive and present in some way, by talking about her endlessly in her absence. The hearts of these children are somewhere else, so their heads are somewhere else too. They cannot concentrate on their school work because they are not really *in* the classroom, in their mind they are with their sorely missed Mummy or Daddy. When children are in a state of yearning like this, people and events around them can quickly become drained of all colour and interest. Everything loses its meaning. Nothing and no one is interesting enough.

Mahler, a psychoanalyst who studied separation anxiety in great depth, says that increasingly, from the age of eighteen months onwards, the infant 'starts to turn away from Mummy and fall in love with the world' (Mahler, 1968). But for some children this is not the case. They cannot fall in love with the world. They cannot feel the loveliness in the world. They can feel only their desperate missing for their parent.

The suffering of missing a parent too much can run very deep. Its intensity may feel unbearable to a child. In effect, such a child can be dragging around too heavy a burden of grief – a desperate and yet often mute cry of 'Come back! Come back!', 'Don't leave me! Don't leave me!' Moreover, for young children who have no sense of time, the present can feel like forever. As an example, a mother told her three-year-old that she would be away for a week. The little girl said, 'So will you be back by one o'clock today to have lunch with me?'

For some children, their longing and yearning for Mummy or Daddy makes the world seem not just bleak, but at times actually hostile. A motherless place in a child's mind can all too easily evoke a sense of a cold, rejecting, unfriendly world outside.

**Siege**

I drag about this thirst for you, your absence
Blaring out a pain of savage poverty;
My mind a stare of lack, a tomb of rotting yesterdays
Their callous echoes mounting to a yell that throws
Its shock, its slap of loss, dislodging everything
Unsteadies everything, all hope into a slump
Of something too snuffed out.

The light dies here.

And now you tread yourself into my grief
Like a vandal, intent to smash this too frail self
Which splinters with the thud of yearning.
No dawn, no bright of dawn,
Just some lost river, in a land already parched and black

I cannot cry you out of me.

*Margot Sunderland*

# Understanding why children yearn

## Children who yearn because they cannot light up the person they love

> For my mother, who loved only 'priceless things', there was nothing on the market within my reach. The door to her happiness was, therefore, closed to me . . . My love was not, apparently, the right key. (Cardinal, 1993, p70)

In the story, Frog has an undying loyalty to the moon, a faithful love in the face of her non-response to him. He just wants to light up the moon, to see her smile *because of him*. Because she had smiled at him once, he now spends all his life sitting waiting, in case she does so once more. By clinging to her with his eyes – thus clinging to his hope that he will eventually light her up – little Frog gets farther and farther away from satisfying that hope.

Frog's story represents one of the most emotionally painful experiences there is for a child: desperately wanting someone who does not want him, or desperately loving someone who does not love him. Some children keep trying to get someone to love them who cannot love them because that person is too damaged or too defended as a result of *their own* painful childhood experience.

Imagine: on too many occasions, a baby looks up into his mother's eyes, and finds that they cannot meet his – or finds something too dead in them, something too unlit, something that holds no delight in looking back at him. He stretches his arms towards her, but she puts him down without responding. Or a five-year-old boy who repeatedly tries to please Daddy by bringing him paintings, things he has found, and work that he has done at school. But, however hard he tries, he feels only his father's disappointment in him.

If a child feels that his love is not valued, is unnoticed or unreciprocated, he concludes that he is basically unlovable – sometimes even repellent, to this most important person in his life. He may be left feeling that there must be something terribly wrong with him; that he is too greedy, too needy, too demanding or utterly undesirable. If his love is rejected like this time after time, what has he left to give his parent? What has he left to bring to the world? He has lost his essential goodness. He is rendered worthless. He is a nothing.

The psychoanalyst Fairbairn describes the infant whose love is unreciprocated as 'exploding ineffectively'. It is as if all his loving feelings just fall into the space between him and his loved one and then are lost. His world becomes utterly bleak.

> His . . . love of his mother, in the face of rejection at her hands . . . is equivalent to discharging his love into an emotional vacuum. Such a discharge is accompanied by an [emotional] experience which is singularly devastating. In the older child this experience is one of intense humiliation over the depreciation of his love, which seems to be involved. At a somewhat deeper level (or at an earlier stage) the experience is one of shame over the display of needs that are disregarded or belittled. By virtue of these experiences of humiliation and shame [the baby] feels reduced to a state of worthlessness, destitution or beggardom. His sense of his own value is threatened: and he feels bad in the sense of 'inferior'. At a still deeper level (or at a still earlier stage) the child's experience is one of, so to speak, exploding ineffectively . . . It is thus an experience of disintegration and of imminent psychical death. (Fairbairn, 1952, p113)

It is important to add, however, that for many children emotional indifference or rebuffal from a parent is rarely likely to be total. There will be times when she does smile at him, hold him close, tell him stories. But this can cause all the more pain. The child remembers times when his mother *was* loving, and because of this it makes the times of non-response or uninterest, or the 'slap' of her disappointment, even more painful and bleak in contrast.

> A deeper and even more dreadful experience – the experience of the faceless mother, that is, the mother whose face does not light up at the sight of her child. (Kohut, 1984, p21)

## Infant-mother research about babies lighting up their mothers

A baby aged four-and-a-half months is seen with his mother: 'Her smile triggers a smile in him and breathes a vitality into him . . . His joy rises. Her smile pulls it out of him. Then Joey himself fully releases it from inside; "I quicken. My sails fill with her. The dance within me is set free".' (Stern, 1990, p65) (Stern is a central figure in infant–mother research.)

Infant–mother research shows that from two to six months old, faces are a baby's main interest and focus, particularly the faces of his parents. During this time, in good infant–mother relationships, there are intense periods of eye contact, smiling, and rich sounds and gurgling conversations. It is only later that the baby begins to become interested in toys. Stern therefore views this early period in life as one of the most intensely social periods of anyone's life.

Videos (Murray, 1988, p159) detailing second-by-second interaction between mother and child show how, when the mother's loving gaze is not forthcoming, the baby tries hard to get her to look at him. He will try to make his mother come alive to him and respond. If she does not, or only responds mechanically, he will eventually stop trying and give up. If this happens time after time, he is likely to appear lifeless, lethargic and pudding-like. In short, such babies are not naturally lit up with love of life. The parent has to light up the baby. To do this, the baby needs to see the light in his mother's face, lit up with her delight in him.

Tragically, some children who had 'faceless' mothers when they were babies continue to exhibit very withdrawn or apathetic behaviour in their school years. This may endure into adulthood. Some children appear to move on from this tragedy (often repressed and forgotten) of having failed to light up their very first love (their mother or father), yet often the grief can be seen deep in their eyes. Moreover, there are usually major scars on their self-esteem.

A very moving paper, 'The Importance of Beauty in Psychoanalytic Experience' (Reid, 1990), is about a boy aged two who was so emotionally 'dead' that at one time he was labelled autistic. Since birth, he had had an awful relationship with his mother, in whose face he never saw any love for him. His mother used to carry him around in a plastic bag. She had psychotic episodes, and heard voices telling her that he was bad and that she had to injure him, which she did. As a result, the little boy would relate to no one, but would lie on the floor face-down. In fact he very nearly died. His hair fell out and he was continually dangerously ill. He had, in effect, given up, just as babies in orphanages will die in their first year of life if fed and watered but given no love, or warm and tender human contact (see Montagu, 1971, especially Chapter 4; also Spitz, 1941).

When the boy went into therapy (at the age of two), he started to come to life. It happened quite dramatically in a session when he suddenly saw the light in his therapist's face when she smiled at him. He knew that it was her affection for him that had lit up her face. Immediately, he became transfixed by the lights in the room. He then went around finding the building (in reality somewhat shabby) a source of wonder, and the people in it very beautiful. He had come alive. He now wanted to live. He had lit up his therapist's face, and on seeing this, he became lit up.

> The mother, then reveals by the light and expression on her face, the nature of the baby in her mind, which is there to be read by the baby and which forms the basis for his developing self-image from the beginning of life. (Reid, 1990, p48)

## Stories told by children who felt they could not light up their mother or their father

**Patsy, aged six**

Having told a story of a bleak house Patsy said, 'I don't like things that don't shine properly, like bare light-bulbs. And sometimes the sky gets so horribly dull and horribly grey too.' Patsy's mother had suffered from clinical depression for many years.

**Duncan, aged eight**

Duncan said that his main feeling was boredom. Later he said, 'Dad and me don't talk any more.' Duncan spoke in a dull, monotonous voice, as if giving out the message that he was not worth listening to. His best friend had just left him for, he said, 'a more interesting friend'. So Duncan was regrettably recreating in his peer relationships his lifeless interactions with his very tired, overburdened single father. Duncan's stories usually included some kind of cliff-face: 'The climber is trying to get a handhold, but he keeps falling off.'

**Toby, aged six**

At the beginning of counselling, Toby said, 'I'm rubbish. I've always known it.' Toby had never been able to light up his mother, who had suffered from severe post-natal depression and never really bonded with him after that. But he was seen as lovely in the eyes of his counsellor. He started to take this in. So, by the end of the counselling, Toby made up a story of a magnificent bird. He said, 'The coloured bird is beautiful. Toby is beautiful.' It was the birth of a 'loved self'.

**Mark, aged eight**

Mark's mother put him into care. She said she did not love him any more because he was so naughty. Mark told a story of an Egyptian mummy with her arms cut off. (A poignant metaphor of how his mother no longer reached out to him.)

**Angela, aged four**

Angela's mother said in front of her that she did not want her. Angela's story: 'There was nothing the tortoise could do but die.' Everything was either dead or drowning in her stories.

**Sascha, aged seven**

Sascha drew his mother as the sun, then drew himself in the middle of the sun. But Sascha's mother was a mother who could not actually warm him as no one had warmed her when *she* was a little girl. He made up a song called 'I am really awful'.

> **Sammy, aged five**
> Sammy's father had left and his mother was very busy. Sammy told a story of a playground, but it was deserted. 'The swings are lonely too,' he said.

## The absence in the presence: children who yearn for a parent who seems unreachable, although she is right there

> One cannot attend to . . . screams successfully without finding out how they are heard. (Jackson, 1992, p16)

Some children yearn for a parent who is an 'absent presence'. This means that their parent is there physically, but, at crucial moments, emotionally absent. In other words, they are there but also 'not there'. Sometimes the parent is just too preoccupied with her own feelings to be fully there for the feelings of her children, or too preoccupied with life's troubles to pay her child enough quality attention. She may be too defeated about life to 'bring to life' someone else. She may be acting out of duty rather than love, unable to feel moved by her child. She may be completely unaware that she is not giving the child something he so desperately needs, because of her own emotionally bleak childhood. Or she may have failed to bond with her child because of too many severed bonds in her own life, and too much ungrieved loss. For some parents, intimacy with anyone is just too painful, and this can extend to their own child.

Whatever the reason, being with a parent who is too often emotionally 'somewhere else', can often be far more lonely and tormenting for a child than having no one there at all. *Real* absence is often far easier to handle than *absent presence*. Indeed, babies and children are acutely able to pick up when their mothers are physically with them, but emotionally somewhere else. Furthermore, when a child has a too often 'absent present' Mummy, the times and glimpses of the emotionally present loving Mummy that he so desperately craves, can feed his addiction, yearning and agonised need for her.

A parent can, of course, feel all the pain and guilt of not being able to give to her child the loving responsiveness she knows he so badly needs. She may be all too painfully aware that she cannot find enough 'desire' in herself to play regularly with her child; talk to him; cuddle him; gaze at him with interest and delight; tell him stories; sing to him; stay close while he falls asleep; or let him fall asleep in her arms. Too often, she may find herself unable to give willingly or naturally because no one in *her* life is adequately emotionally nourishing *her*. No one in her life is helping her with *her* feelings. It may also be that her own inner child was never lovingly parented either.

Parental guilt is often prevalent in post-natal depression, where mothers may feel all the agony of knowing that they have more rejecting (and sometimes murderous) feelings towards their baby than the expected loving ones. They may then live with the pain of knowing that they often feel like withdrawing from their baby, rather than approaching him with delight.

Sometimes it is the infant's desperate level of need, or the anguish in his crying, that triggers too much of a mother's own unmet infantile need or infantile pain. So she turns away from him, or deadens her responsiveness to him as he is unintentionally holding up a mirror to a part of herself that is too unbearable for her to feel again. All this can happen completely out of her conscious awareness.

**Post-Natal Depression**

Why do you hate what you have birthed
And dread the little clinging bones
Which once you held so tightly to your breast
What vileness did you find in him
Which made you gag and snatch life back,
Like some too brutal bailiff
With all the shudder of unannounced,
Ripping him out to reclaim you.

And as you turn to favoured ones,
He is a flicked off fleck of thing
That slips from both your mind and arms
To some cold floor for outcast fools
Strewn, with the dry cracks of his resigned knowing
That he'll *always* lose his place in you.

You do not feel the separation,
It is of no significance.
To you it is a nothing gap,
To him it is his death.

*Margot Sunderland*

**Stories told by children who have yearned for an unreachable parent:**

**Zack, aged six**

Zack's Mummy loved Zack for the first three months of his life. She then lost her own mother and sank into an awful depression which included, she said, falling out of love with Zack. She said she felt awful about it, but could only respond to Zack from a sense of duty.

*Story one:* 'Little fox is always trying to get to Mummy fox, but there are too many obstacles in the way – monsters, and too high walls and crocodile-infested rivers. So he never gets to her.'

*Story two:* 'The chipmunk has travelled by mistake to the far ends of the earth. His Mummy tries to find him on a big sailing boat but there is no wind, so it never gets to him. Then she goes by car, but the car runs out of petrol.'

Zack's stories are all about failed or lost connections. Indeed, Zack cannot reach the loving part of his mother, and yet he goes on searching and searching for it. Like Frog, Zack had seen the moon (mother) smile at him for the first three months of his life. So he is left in a state of searching to find in her once more what he has so tragically lost.

**Charlie, aged eight**

Charlie had an alcoholic mother. She was addicted to her drink. Charlie was addicted to her.

'There's this funny little toad, who spends his day trying to eat chewing-gum that's got stuck on the floor. He drinks from puddles and eats from dustbins. In fact, all the animals are just too hungry like that.'

**Melody, aged twelve**

Melody's mother said that when Melody was a baby she had often left her to cry. (She had read the baby books that said this was the right thing to do.) Melody had regularly made herself physically sick from so much crying and calling for her Mummy.

'Even if the little moth throws itself against the light again and again, it can't get the light to say hello. But it still keeps throwing itself against the light.' It was true that even when Melody had thrown herself against her mother (metaphorically) again and again with her crying, she could not get a response.

**Tammie, aged eight**

Sadly, Tammie was not able to reach her depressed single mother. At school, nobody wanted to play with Tammie. (She came over as too hungry, too clingy, desperate for their friendship, and they recoiled when they felt her desperation.) In the story Tammie made up, she told of a place called 'sad': 'Sad is lonely. Lonely is fog, and fog is too still'. She also made up a story about a 'What's the point Play-Doh blob?', but it got all muddled up with a lonely Play-Doh blob.

*Another of Tammie's stories:* 'The swamps take me down into their hole of gloom.' When asked what she'd like to say to the swamps, she said, 'Don't take me to your deadly dark, you wouldn't like it.' Tammie felt sucked down and down by her mother's depression.

**Picture of a child who fell out of his Mummy's mind**

Today he fell out of her mind
Her arms became too limp and long
He fell right down the front of her,
Got all-torn-up and paper-binned.

Now searching for his littered self,
He walks among his dreadful grief
And finds a lethal world of just-himself,
There is no lovely here.

He longs
That she might read the calling of his eyes
*remember me, remember me,*
That she might see
*just once,*
And feel his falling from her mind
Yet has no words to speak of how he'd tried to cling
But helpless, lost his grip
And blown away like little dust.

He only wanted life,
He could not find it without her.

*Margot Sunderland*

## 'She loves me, she loves me not': children who yearn because they have a parent who is loving one minute and rejecting the next

> For a young child the experience . . . of losing [his mother's] love is in very truth a bereavement. (Bowlby, 1978, p33)

Some parents are loving or exciting one minute, and rejecting or indifferent the next. This is known as *intermittent reinforcement*. It all too easily leads to the child having an addiction to that parent. This was demonstrated in a famous experiment with rats. When a peanut regularly and consistently came down a chute, the rats could soon move away from the chute. When a peanut never came down the chute, they ignored it. When a peanut came down the chute unpredictably – sometimes it did and sometimes it did not – the rats were transfixed by the chute and could not move away from it.

The pain of having had something (the moon *did* once smile at Frog) then losing it, can be far worse than never having had it or known it at all, because then you know exactly what you are missing. One adolescent client in therapy described his relationship with his on-off mother as being like a yoyo, as a constant switch between pure heaven and then just desert: 'It was like I kept falling out of the Garden of Eden', he said. This form of loss can also be experienced as a betrayal: having enjoyed blissful intimacy together one minute, to being coldly or sharply treated or turned away from the next. The change from 'hot' to 'cold' and back again can happen over any timescale. For some children, for example, the change from meeting a warm loving mother to meeting a cold or indifferent one can happen from minute to minute. For others, they may meet a loving mother one day, and a cold one the next; or a cold and angry one in the morning, who is then fine and loving in the afternoon.

A child may have shared some exquisitely beautiful moments with his mother; known that he could really light her up with delight in him – but then at other times found her cold, rejecting or indifferent. Or perhaps he has had many beautiful moments with his mother, but they were just too precarious, too temporary, too fleeting. So, momentarily, he is filled with hope, but then, when the light goes out in her for him, everything lovely in his world is too abruptly gone. There is the hope of a connection, but then it is smashed, as she has withdrawn from him in some way. Then there can be the death of hope, which for some children brings a deep despair.

Imagine a baby whose mother is emotionally cold, after she has been warm and loving. She picks up her baby from a place of duty in herself rather than a place of warmth and love. She does not understand why he is not comforted. Although he is physically close, he is crying because he cannot find the Mummy he is looking for. It is as if in his desperate state he is saying, 'Mummy, I can't find you! I can only find a dead version of you. I'm desperate to find the warm, loving Mummy and I can only find this cold lifeless one.' The 'death' of response in his mother can feel like a death in him, hence the intense pain his cries express.

This is a common vicious cycle: the more empty of loving, comfort and warmth a tired or overstretched mother is at any time, the more desperate and inconsolable the baby can become. Mothers may not understand that their baby often screams without let-up, not because of physical pain or discomfort, but because they give him a flat, mechanical or preoccupied response. It is as if in his crying, which at such times becomes a calling, he is searching in a hall of mirrors for his alive mother, but he just keeps finding illusions of her – dead, jarring or frightening illusions. And sometimes, the more desperate he becomes, the more his mother feels desperate too, at the end of her tether and, in that moment, a failure as a mother. She feels attacked by her feelings of inadaquecy, of which he is the source. So she withdraws from him even more. If only during these trying times the mother can keep *something* about her alive and warm and tender, then the desperate infant will be able to connect with her again. If she can hold him to her in a tender way, or keep her voice alive with love and warmth, he will be comforted. He just needs *some* sense that his loving Mummy is there.

## Children who yearn because they suffer from separation anxiety

I searched for Mum till my eyes hurt with too much looking and my head spun with too much exertion. Then, suddenly, with the sun burning itself into evening, with so many people around, everyone active, everything moving, I was overcome with a strange panic. I couldn't see a single familiar face in that jostling universe. And then just as suddenly, in flashes of lighting and dark, I began to see Mum everywhere. (Okri, 1991, p162)

The following is an official psychiatric description of the central features of separation anxiety:

● Recurrent excessive distress when separation from home or major attachment figures occurs or is anticipated.

● Persistent and excessive worry about losing, or about possible harm befalling major attachment figures.

● Persistent and excessive worry that an untoward event will lead to separation from a major attachment figure (eg, getting lost or being kidnapped).

● Persistent reluctance or refusal to go to school or elsewhere because of fear of separation.

● Persistently and excessively fearful, or reluctant to be alone or without major attachment figures at home or without significant adults in other settings.
(American Psychiatric Association, 1994, p113).

Separation anxiety means that, when apart from a person you love, you feel very anxious, often fearing that you will never see that person again; never be reunited; that something awful will happen to your loved one in the time apart. If a child suffers from separation anxiety, he also often conceives of time as something that will only take away, it will not bring back again in the future (whereas, logically speaking, time *has* to take away, to be used up, in order to bring back the person in the future). So for a child who is troubled in this way, being separated from Mummy can become the world of Romeo and Juliet, the child fearing that, 'If I am separated from Mummy, I may never find her again.'

At the age of four or five, some children go to school for the first time with anxiety, but they manage it. Others, who suffer from acute separation anxiety, are in a desperate state of fear or panic. School-age children who suffer like this have not yet developed a state of inner security from which they actively want to move away from Mummy to explore the world (as long as they can keep coming back to her to refuel!). If they never reach this state of emotional security, separation anxiety can remain, if untreated, in some form right into adulthood.

In adults, separation anxiety is often disguised in some neurotic symptom, such as agoraphobia. The anxiety is transferred from leaving mother then, to leaving their house now. Going on holiday or on a journey can retrigger all manner of childhood separation anxieties. So, when an adult (or part of them) just wants to stay at home, it is often a kind of unconscious infantile clinging, clinging to their home as mother-substitute. There are all manner of mother-substitutes: 'I can't separate from my alcohol, my smoking, my drugs, my anti-depressants, I cling on to them for dear life. Just think of the despair [the blackness in *The Frog who Longed for Moon*] if I didn't !'

We will look now at circumstances that can bring about such painful feelings of insecurity. If a child has 'internalised' a strong, calm, utterly reliable 'mother world', this image of her can be carried inside him wherever he goes. The mother in his mind is loving, warm and consistently there for him. He will feel fundamentally safe in being in the world; not only safe when actually with his Mummy or significant other person. In contrast, a child without this sort of mother in his head does not feel safe when he actually *is* safe, because the feeling of safety is not inside him.

### Children who suffer from separation anxiety because at some point Mummy was away too long

Some children suffer from separation anxiety because, at some time in their young life, Mummy was away too long. For example, Tommy, aged six said: 'When I'm not next to my Mummy, I'm always in the wrong place.' Tommy had been put into care for a while when he was a year old, as his mother was hospitalised. He had become very clingy, and sometimes intensely angry at her.

The psychoanalyst Bowlby (1978), has documented in great depth what happens when children under five are separated from their mothers for too long. He details the common reaction of a desperate yearning and searching. As Kaplan explains, 'A baby's confidence includes the idea that his actual mother, the mother-in-the-flesh, will stay put' (1978, p125).

When babies start to explore and to crawl, you can see that they always come back to their mother-base before venturing out again. The young infant who starts to move about cannot correctly locate himself in space without a solid 'mother place' to keep returning to. The space without a mother, therefore, becomes extremely frightening and dangerous.

> Distance is meaningless to a young child unless it is distance from someone with whom he has a dialogue. Deprived of the beacon of a mother's presence, a child has no place to return to, no way to imagine how far or where to creep or walk. There is no exhilaration or joy in moving the body. Instead the child falls and bumps into the objects of the out-there world in a desperate attempt to locate the edges of his body and the boundaries of his world. (Kaplan, 1978, p124)

If Mummy is away too long and the infant is left with someone with whom he does not have a strong attachment, this motherless space can be unbearably painful and frightening. He may cry bitterly; try to search for her in some way; yearn for her terribly; talk about her endlessly to anyone who will listen, or look at the door through which she left, not taking his eyes off it. His grief will deepen. After a while he may stop crying (as crying is a calling and a protest), and go into despair.

The Robertsons (psychologists working in the 1950s and 1960s) made films of one- and two-year-olds. The films show the trauma these children suffered when Mummy was away for over a week or so having a baby. The films became very famous. They made it all too clear that separating infants from parents for too long (when they were not left with someone with whom they had a strong attachment), was very damaging. The films were shown to psychiatrists and hospital staff all over the world. One film called 'John' (available from Concord Films) shows John missing his Mummy very much and suffering from the acutest of separation anxiety. He slowly gives up, psychologically dies, and refuses to eat, until, at the end of nine days, he lies in a lifeless heap on the floor. It is a very distressing film and yet it served to change attitudes towards childcare across the world.

When Mummy does come back after being away too long, the child may have detached himself from her because of too much pain. He may look straight through her; seem not to recognise her or even struggle to get away from her. After a period of time with her, however, if she is lucky, he may break out of this and start a new phase with her of going into desperate clinging, not wanting to let her out of his sight and following her everywhere. All now depends on her response as to whether things will be mended between them or not. Can she bear her child's initial rebuttal of her? Can she bear his then desperate period of clinging and not wanting to let her out of his sight, in case she goes away again? The damage will be minimised if:

✧ She is able to understand and empathise with his reactions.

✧ She is able to deal with his clinging and following her around, without punishing him or pushing him away, calling him weak, babyish and so on.

✧ She can understand that he needs to cling simply because he does not feel secure enough yet to let go of her again.

✧ With older children, she is able to listen, and bear the child's intense, frightened, enraged and hurting feelings about her having gone away without impatience, frustration or going into 'That's enough now, dear'.

If the mother does not understand about the intense feelings provoked by a broken connection between them, the child is unlikely to get the empathic response he so desperately needs to repair both himself and their relationship. If, for example, he is pushed away for clinging too much; or criticised for his healthy protesting anger at being left (which may come out in all manner of acting out behaviour); or if he is met with a cold or indifferent face when he has been desperately yearning for her, then it is likely that things will not be mended. As a result, something may die in the child. Moreover, difficulties with loving, intimacy and close relationships in later life are likely to be his legacy from this traumatic time.

---

**Rupert, aged three**

Rupert's mother had frequently been away in hospital when he was a baby. For years in his early childhood, Rupert used to wake up several times a night, distraught, crying, 'I've lost my teddy!'; 'I've lost my blanket!'; 'I've lost my truck!' They were in fact right by him, and sometimes he was even holding them. He would 'lose' them repeatedly throughout the night, and the same thing would happen all over again. His parents were exhausted, and started to get irritated. They failed him by calling him attention-seeking, rather than trying to understand his underlying communication to them, which was all about the frantic desperation states that can result from the intolerable loss of a broken connection.

---

Where a mother is unable to deal with or even see her child's pain and grief in response to her absence, it is often because, when *she herself* was a child, *her own* desperate states of infantile need or longing were not met with sufficient compassion and understanding.

## 'The Mummy in my mind': children who yearn because they did not make a strong enough connection with Mummy before she left for the day

Sometimes a child can spend all day at nursery or school pining for Mummy because she left him before he felt 'full of her'. If his last connection with his Mummy is too faint, a child can be left with a too-faint Mummy in his mind. If his last connection is with a preoccupied Mummy, he can be left with a preoccupied Mummy in his mind. Or, worse, if she turns away and does not acknowledge him in any way, his mind can be empty of a loving Mummy.

When there is a poor, too faint, or broken connection between them, there can be little or no comfort to be had in any comforter or transitional object (such as cloth, a scarf or a teddy which symbolises her). This comforter now becomes just a painful reminder of what he has lost – rather than a lovely reminder of what he *has* (the inner image of a loving mother).

In contrast, if a child's last connection with his mother was a loving one in which he felt lovingly held in both her mind and her arms, then that is the mother he keeps with him during the day. He can bathe in delicious memories of her and him together. Such memories glow inside him; hold his sense of self steady, and can make the world feel a very good place to be.

## Children who yearn because the time they do have with Mummy is too snatched

In the story, Frog is clinging with all his attention to the moon. He has no wish to explore the world around him. Because Frog has not drunk in enough of the moon's loving response to him, he cannot leave her. She has just given him emotional crumbs, and this has fuelled his need for more. Similarly, snatched time with a too busy or too preoccupied Mummy, rather than time that brings interactions of real warmth and love and shared enjoyment, can engender feelings of desperate need, and a deep insecurity. Children who have drunk in enough good Mummy, metaphorically speaking, can be fine in her absence for the day. 'The secure child in adulthood feels confident and competent, wants to explore, feels bold in his explorations of the world' (Bowlby, 1988, p124). But if they have not, they can be obsessed with her and, psychologically speaking, remain too linked to her.

If you give a starving person titbits they will be obsessed with food. Give them a full meal, and they will be able to move away from the table and get on with their life. When a child has not established a strong loving connection with his mother, the last thing he will feel like doing when it is time to separate is to move away from her and take an interest in exploring the world. Rather, all his energies are focused on wanting to find her and be with her again. As one little boy, who had a very preoccupied mother and so could not experience her as a secure base, said, 'The little tortoise needs help with being lost.'

## Children who yearn because they have experienced too many severings and ruptures

Schore – a neurobiologist and psychotherapist studying infant-mother interactions – says that some of the most painful feelings for infants come from times of disengagements and re-engagements which are badly handled (Schore, 1998). A mother may leave her baby too abruptly in his cot, so he feels dropped or ripped from her, rather than put down. The baby who cries out and has no reply is indeed lost in space and time, so if his mother physically disappears or breaks contact with him in some way, he can feel he has lost her forever and that he will not be able to find her again. Consider the following:

---

**Tessa, aged five**

Tessa was in a desperate state at leaving her mother each day to go to school, frantically clinging, and often physically sick with distress. Her mother tried to deal with this by leaving Tessa quickly, but this made Tessa even more desperate. When Tessa was a baby, her mother used to put her down to sleep in the afternoons to 'establish a routine', although Tessa was not always tired. Tessa used to scream and scream to be picked up, but her mother had read child-care books which said that to give in meant that she was letting her baby control her. The books said that routines were vital. Later when Tessa was two, her mother sent her to spend two weeks with a relative she did not know well. Tessa missed her mother dreadfully. Now all the intensity of Tessa's need from these traumatic times in infancy kept being triggered whenever she had to leave her mother to go to school.

Tessa was offered therapy. It was clear from the therapy, when Tessa kept making up stories of things which kept getting 'broken', and places where everything falls out of everything that Tessa had suffered traumatic ruptures during times of separation from her mother.

---

Through family therapy, Tessa's mother learned to hold Tessa calmly and soothingly during their separations, and then to leave her very slowly, so that Tessa did not retrigger painful feelings of rupture. During Tessa's clinging, her mother tried to remain very calm and unhurried. Eventually, when Tessa had drunk in enough of her mother's absolutely centred, all-the-time-in-the-world feeling of 'being there for her' in a soothing and totally non-rupturing way, she could let her mother go far more easily on school mornings. It was all done through a calm mother state. In fact, soon the leavings often took little more than five minutes.

**Sheetal, aged four**

Sheetal's Mummy did everything very quickly, including her endings with Sheetal. Sheetal said with great sadness, 'When my Mummy leaves me, there's not a Mummy and a Sheetal any more.' This is true, for there is not a 'Mummy-and-a-Sheetal' in her mind any more.

## Children who cling because they were stopped from clinging when they needed to

There had been a blue dress. His fingers had gripped the hem of it. And sometimes his fingers would be removed by other larger fingers, the nails of which resembled large drops of shiny blood. (Cook, 1991, p43)

Many problems of clinging and yearning originate from the natural dependency stage of child development. At this stage, some parents feel too disturbed by the often sheer intensity of infantile need. So out of fear (usually unacknowledged), a parent may try to push her child into independence before he is ready. In so doing, she does not allow the child's natural separation process to happen in its own time. It is sometimes that the needy, totally dependent part of her baby triggers the pain of her own unmet infantile need. Or she may simply be over-stretched, with too many children or demands, and not enough emotional support from the people in her life. Bowlby explains how, in order for a mother to be able to provide a really secure base for her child, someone must be providing a secure base for *her*. There must be someone to soothe, nourish and comfort her, listen to her feelings. How can anyone effectively emotionally feed someone else, when they themselves are emotionally undernourished or emotionally starving?

Some parents, in attempts to prevent clinginess, push the child away when he is in a state of need, or wanting comfort and closeness. Paradoxically, in so doing, by frustrating the need, they actually increase its intensity. So if the child's clinginess is met by impatience, rejection or annoyance, the child is likely to become *more* clingy, or instead to cut off his need, harden his heart and build up a big tough armour that can last a lifetime. Again, this parental failure often occurs because the parent has a difficult relationship with her own dependency needs. (This can be completely out of her awareness.)

Research (Main, 1977; Bowlby, 1988, p49) also shows that infants who, by the age of one are clingy, are often those who were left to cry too long. Hence the parent's deprivation of response is again actually feeding their child's addiction to it. Similarly, research shows that the most secure children are the ones who 'during early infancy, are held longest in a tender and loving way' (Ainsworth *et al*, 1978; Bowlby, 1988, p15), and that immediately responsive mothers do not get clingy or 'difficult' babies.

## What the research says about children who cling

By the end of the first year, mothers who had attended promptly to their crying babies had babies who cried much less than those of mothers who had left them to cry (Bowlby, 1988, p49). So if you want a clingy baby, leave him to cry too long.

Some people think that a child becomes clingy because he has been loved *too much*, or 'spoilt', or had such a good time with Mummy that now he does not want to go to school. This is totally incorrect: 'Despite its wide popularity, no evidence of substance has ever been presented to support the theory that anxious attachment is a result of an excess of parental affection' (Bowlby, 1973, p239).

When children feel very secure with their Mummy, they will naturally start to turn away and explore the world for ever-increasing lengths of time. Research also shows that clinginess is far more likely where a parent has not handled the child's dependency needs well: the parent may have pushed the child to be independent when he was actually feeling very dependent, and needing to be very, very close.

Some children appear clingy, when in fact they have clingy mothers! Some parents are full of their own unmet infantile dependency needs. When they were children, they were what is known as 'anxiously attached' children, because their own parents did not deal well with their dependency needs. So now such parents (usually totally unconsciously) project their dependency needs on to their own child. This means that they may complain that their child is clinging to them, when actually it is they who are clinging to their child!

## Children who yearn because they have been put into care, fostered or adopted

> When you lost things, it was like you only knew for the first time that you'd ever had them. Took a mother's leaving for you to know she'd ever been there, because otherwise she was that place, everything, like weather. (Gibson, 1993, p161)

'If you do that again, I'm going to send you away': the parent who threatens to abandon her child, as a form of control or punishment, is endangering that child's fundamental feeling of safety in the world. Research (Bowlby, 1988) shows that parents using threats to abandon their child as a means of control have an enormously powerful effect, and can cause acute separation anxiety. If a child is *actually* abandoned or sent away, the legacy of grief can be intolerable. It is not surprising, therefore, that such children often move into a world of denial – a clung-to belief that one day Mummy will come back, and everything will be wonderful. This can, of course, mean that in many ways the child cannot get on with his life because he is always on some level, yearning for his 'Mummy back with me again' future.

So, for the child who has been fostered, adopted or put into care, the absent mother can take on fairy-tale proportions. Even if beaten, abused or severely neglected by that parent before she left, the child can still glamorise her in his mind, so strong is a child's need to believe that he has a loving mother. As with Frog, it is too much to give up that belief. As a child, how can you ever really face the fact that your mother does not want you to be with her any more? It is a too terrible reality.

Children who are adopted, fostered or in care who are obsessed with their mother are still expressing hope in their yearning. One little boy put into care would run away on a regular basis and hide in his mother's garden. He would gaze up, just like Frog, at her closed windows. This obsession, addiction and yearning for the absent mother can continue for years. Like Frog these yearning children give the moon (their mother) full attention, while 'the moon' may be giving them very little, if anything, in return. Such children cling to the memory and image in their head of the mother who has left them and fantasise about how they will be reunited with her one day. This yearning can lead to self-accusations such as, 'If I had tried harder to be nice, Daddy would have stayed', or, 'If I hadn't been so naughty, Mummy would not have sent me away.'

The following are stories told by children who yearn because they have been fostered, adopted or put into care:

---

**Sue, aged six**

Sue's mother could not cope, so she was fostered.
*Sue's story:* 'This story is called "When My Mum Comes Back". When my Mum comes back she'll make me a big cake, because she missed my birthday – and then she'll put fruit and candles on the table, and then she'll watch me blow them out.'

Her Mum never came back. In fact, she moved away. With a new, loving foster mother, Sue was able to grieve for her mother in therapy, and was able eventually to love again.

---

**Bella, aged seven**

Bella was left by her mother, an alcoholic.
Bella kept telling stories about roads going nowhere. But they did not come from anywhere, either. The metaphor was very clear: nothing joined up with anything, just as Bella felt traumatically 'unjoined up' to her mother. 'If you go along one of the roads, you come from nowhere and go to nowhere,' Bella said. She could express her hope verbally: 'One day, Mummy will want me again', but her underlying sense of futility came out in her stories.

---

**Lily, aged six**

Lily had been adopted at age two.

Lily's story: 'Nobody wanted the little dolls any more, so they left the playroom and lived on a rubbish dump. The dump was struck by lightning, so they knocked on the door of Mum's house, but Mum turned them away. So they went to a bus shelter, but the bus shelter was struck by lightning . . . so they went to the shops, but all the shops were closed.'

**Bobby, aged ten**

Bobby's mother says, 'I love him, but I don't like him.' When she finds Bobby too much, she sends him to stay with her sister for long periods of time. Bobby often says he wishes he was dead. He has no self-esteem, and no friends.

Bobby's story: 'There's a town where all the houses are rotting; no one lives in them. The silence is dreadful.'

**Toby, aged seven**

Toby's mother puts Toby into care from time to time.

Toby's stories are all about wolves pacing around restlessly in the night: 'Why are the wolves howling? I think they are howling for their mother.'

# Children who yearn for a parent who has died

For some children whose parents have died, the pain of the grief is so unbearable that it must be defended against. But some brave children dare to stay open to the yearning, the grieving and the emptiness. They are deeply bereft. For some children, when they lose a parent, they also lose the hope of there being a warm, kind world. Here are two stories told by bereaved children.

---

**Joby, aged seven**

Joby's mother died when he was six.

He told stories in which 'Babies are suffocating in the sand' and 'My body's gone. It's gone to the empty hungry land' (see Figure 1). In another story, Joby made a heart from Play-Doh, tore it into little bits, then put it in the bin.

---

**Goldie, aged eight**

Goldie's father died a year ago.

Goldie told a story about vases with no flowers, houses with no windows, people with no smiles, and then she said, 'I don't like to do stories if they are sad.' Another time she told this story: 'One day, the sea went out too far, and it never came back. The shells on the beach are waiting for it and waiting for it, because they dare not know that it will never come back. They get all dried up without the water. And what's inside them gets all broken into little dry bitties. And because there is no sea, there is no water any more. It only rains sand.'

---

**Figure 1** Drawing of Joby's sandplay story, 'My body's gone. It's gone to the empty hungry land'. Joby is seven, his mother died when he was six.

# WHAT YOU CAN DO AFTER YOU HAVE READ *THE FROG WHO LONGED FOR THE MOON TO SMILE* TO THE CHILD

This section offers ideas for things to say and do after you have read this story to a child. The tasks, games and exercises are designed specifically to help a child to think about, express and further digest his feelings about the story's theme.

As previously discussed, children often cannot speak clearly and fully in everyday language about what they are feeling, but they can show or enact, draw or play out their feelings. Therefore, many of the exercises in this section offer support for creative, imaginative and playful means of expression. They are also designed to inspire a child to respond further by telling his own stories.

To avoid your asking the child too many questions (children can soon feel interrogated), some exercises just require a tick in a box, or the choosing of a word or image from a selection.

*Please note* The tasks, games and exercises are not designed to be worked through in chronological order. Also, there are far too many to attempt them all in one go – the child could feel bombarded. So just pick the ones you think would be right for the child you are working with, taking into account his age, and how open he is to the subject matter. Instructions to the child are in tinted boxes.

## ☆ Loving without being loved back

Have you ever really loved or liked someone who didn't love or like you back?
Draw what it made you feel.

## ✰ The place of not-enough and the place of more-than-enough

- Make a sand picture or draw 'The Place of Not-Enough', then make a sand picture or draw 'The Place of More-Than-Enough'.
- What do you feel, being in 'The Place of Not-Enough'?
- Pick a miniature figure to be you and put yourself in this place. Show what you do there or say there.
- What do you feel, being in 'The Place of More-Than-Enough'? Pick a miniature figure to be you and put yourself in this place. Show or say what you do there.
- Now, using a miniature figure, tell a story of how you get from 'The Place of Not-Enough' to 'The Place of More-Than-Enough'.

## ✰ The very missed person in your mind

Draw a person you miss very much. Draw how you see them in your mind. Then think, if they were a colour or an object or an animal, what would they be? Draw it.

For example, one child drew a faded Mummy, another drew a patch of fog 'where my Daddy used to be', another drew a tiny Mummy figure as a speck on the horizon: 'She has gone too far out'. A bereaved child drew the Mummy in his mind as a lovely soft pillow.

## ✰ Daring to let go

The next exercise is for the child who is hanging on to someone, who they also want to let go of, because they know the person does not want to be with them any more in any major, loving way.

> ⊚ Imagine a hook, or another kind of bond or join (such as a rope, chains) between you and the person you are hanging on to, but who you want to let go of. Now draw yourself letting go of it in some way. You might like to cut it, or just undo it or loosen it.
>
> ⊚ What do you feel when you let go of this person you are desperately hanging on to in your mind?
>
> ⊚ What are the good things about letting go?
>
> ⊚ What are the bad things about letting go?

## ☆ Some missing-you-too-much words

The next three exercises are about helping children with a language for grief. This is so that they can be enabled to speak about their grief or yearning in richer, more specific ways, rather than just saying that they are sad. The exercises may also help the children to speak about the intensity of their feelings.

*When you miss this person in your life, does the missing feel like any of these? If it does, tick the boxes.*

Feeling lost ☐

Like there's a big hole, or empty space inside you where the person you miss used to be ☐

Desperate ☐

Starving ☐

Empty ☐

Can't really think about anything else ☐

Too much hurt inside ☐

Screaming inside for the person you miss ☐

Silently howling inside for the person you miss ☐

Wanting to cry and cry and cry ☐

Imagining them leaving you all over again ☐

Imagining yourself all cuddled up in them ☐

Like your heart is broken ☐

Fearing you will never see them again ☐

Fearing that something awful will happen to you or them before you meet again ☐

## ✩ What missing too much feels like

- ◉ Draw what it feels like inside you when you are missing this person too much.
- ◉ Draw what it feels like inside your mind.
- ◉ Draw what your heart feels like.
- ◉ Draw, or do a sandplay picture, of how the world feels when you are missing this person too much.
- ◉ Draw, or do a sandplay picture, of how the world feels when you are back together with this person.

## ✩ Tummy-hunger and heart-hunger

- ◉ It is easy to muddle up tummy-hunger with heart-hunger.
- ◉ When your heart is feeling too empty and hurting, it can sometimes feel like it must be your tummy.
- ◉ Draw what you feel when you are too empty inside because you are missing someone too much. Draw what the world feels like when you are too empty inside.

**Terry, aged six**

Terry's mother has severe depression, so he experiences her as emotionally unavailable.

*Terry:* 'The dinosaurs are fighting. They are fighting because they are too hungry.'

*Therapist:* 'Yes, when your heart is hungry, not your tummy, it can make you feel desperate and fighting inside.'

## ✩ The lovely times

The next exercise is for children whose yearned-for person has left or died, but who did feel very loved by them when they were there:

> Draw, or write, or tell of some of the lovely things about the person you miss or some of the lovely times you shared together. You might have hoarded these memories away deep in your mind, but if you talk, or show or draw them, it can help you feel warmer inside. These lovely memories are like treasures, and no one can ever take them away from you. But if you hoard them too deep down in your mind, and don't bring them out, they may get all cobwebby and, like that, they can't warm you.
>
> It's as if you know two worlds at the moment. One is the lovely world you had together, and the lovely moments you shared. The other is the world without that lovely person. It is good to feel your feelings about both worlds. But do it with someone there to listen, so it can feel safe and far less scary and lonely.

## ✩ Loss

The following is a suggestion of what you might say to help a child understand the pain of loss in missing someone, and how it helps to talk about it with someone who can really listen and really know.

> Missing can hurt a lot, just like a broken limb or a cut knee. It often hurts too much. You just want the pain to go away. Physical pain needs medicine. But for emotional pain, the best medicine is telling someone you really like and trust all about how much you hurt and – if you are brave enough – to let yourself cry in front of that person.

## ☆ The 'I'm not-lovable' muddle

Draw what it feels like to you, when you don't feel liked or loved by a very important person in your life. Then draw yourself with that other person. Draw the expression they have on their face. Draw the expression you have on your face.

When you don't feel liked or loved, do you believe that it is because you are unlikeable or unlovable? Did you say to yourself, 'X left because I was unlovable'?

It is very easy to jump to the conclusion that it is *you* who is unlovable, rather than thinking that perhaps the person you want to love you is finding it hard to love *anyone* at the moment, or that they are just not good at loving and caring for children (because of what has happened to them in their lives).

Draw a speech bubble out of your mouth, and write in it what you want to say to this person. If it helps, just finish the sentences:

I am angry with you because _____

I am sad because _____

I am hurt because _____

What I want from you is _____

## ☆ 'And then . . .'

For older children, get them to play the 'And then . . .' game.

The child imagines giving up his addiction to, or obsession with, this person who does not love him back. The therapist or counsellor just helps them explore more and more deeply by saying, 'And then?' after each imagining. For example:

| | |
|---|---|
| *Counsellor:* | 'If I let go of my obsession with this person, I'll . . . ' |
| *Child:* | 'I'll just feel awful and not want to do anything all day but sit in my room . . . ' |
| *Counsellor:* | 'And then?' |
| *Child:* | 'And then I'll sink lower and lower.' |
| *Counsellor:* | 'And then?' |
| *Child:* | 'I will probably feel very bored.' |
| *Counsellor:* | 'And then?' |

| | |
|---|---|
| *Child:* | 'I'll think, "How dare she not like me?", and I'll feel like smashing things up.' |
| *Counsellor:* | 'And then?' |
| *Child:* | 'I'll ring up Ted and see if he wants to go roller-skating with me.' |

At times, this exercise can help children find inner resources they did not know, or had forgotten they had, such as a determination, or a real desire not to waste their lives any more in clinging to a person who does not love them. Or it may give them a reassurance that they can survive what can feel unsurvivable; or even enable them to see the funny side. At other times, it may lead the child further into their despair or grief, but at least you, as therapist, then know what you are dealing with, and these very painful feelings can be addressed, grieved over and worked through.

## ✫ The dark night of the soul, and how to survive it

What to say to an older child about the dark night of the soul, when he dares to stop trying to get someone who cannot love him to love him.

Many people have gone into horrible dark, or painful places when they have given up trying to get someone to like them or love them – but, after a time, when they look back, they see that letting go in this way actually gave them a brand new start, a new direction which was better than the old one they had, and which they might otherwise never have taken. They realise that the relationship they had with that person was not really best for them that it had actually gone wrong in some way, and was causing them too much pain. It's just that they had got used to the pain as a way of living life. Because they dared to let go of someone who didn't love them, or couldn't love them, they then were able to go and find someone who *did* love them.

You can demonstrate all of what you are saying by doing a sand picture for the child, illustrating how, 'When you are facing the gates of hell, you have your back to the gates of heaven'.

# CONSIDERING COUNSELLING OR THERAPY FOR CHILDREN WHO YEARN

**Emma, aged eighteen**

As a child I tried everything to get my father to respond to me – seduction, trying to be perfect, naughtiness, even shooting missiles at the wall. It took me years to let myself feel the despair of not getting through. But once I did, in therapy at the age of twelve, it freed me to be able finally to walk away from his wall – to turn away, and look at the world, instead of all those bricks. I hadn't realised the view could be so beautiful.

Sadly, some children addicted to 'bad-deal' relationships can, without therapeutic intervention, go on as adults to have one bleak, bad-deal relationship after another. In later life, they may find themselves endlessly reliving the non-responsive relationships from their past in their present, or staying in a rejecting relationship, because unconsciously they are still trying to get Daddy or Mummy to love them all over again. Or, if they do find a good Mummy-partner or Daddy-partner, they may cling to them with all their desperate unmet infantile need. This can result in their partner leaving them, and so the trauma is repeated.

A sign of successful therapy with children is that they will want to spend more time with a situation or person that is good for them and away from a situation or person that is neglecting, abusive or depriving. Before therapy, children addicted to bad-deal relationships often turn away from loving relationships.

Therapy or counselling is vital for children who have suffered a major loss or bereavement, and who have no one in their lives with whom they can really mourn. Without such a person, a child may find the intensity of the pain too much, and so cut himself off and harden his heart. This is a drastic defence, which can mean that in later life he may never dare to love again.

# BIBLIOGRAPHY

**Ainsworth MDS, Blehar MC, Waters E & Wall S,** 1978, *Patterns of Attachment: A Psychological Study of The Strange Situation,* Lawrence Erlbaum Associates, Hillsdale, NJ.

**American Psychiatric Association,** 1994, *Diagnostic and Statistical Manual of Mental Disorders: DSM-IV,* 4th edn, American Psychiatric Association, Washington.

**Armstrong-Perlman EM,** 1991, 'The Allure of the Bad Object', *Free Associations,* 2 (3)23: 343–56.

**Balint E,** 1993, *Before I Was I: Psychoanalysis and the Imagination,* eds J Mitchell & M Parsons, Free Association Books, London.

**Bowlby J,** 1973, *Attachment and Loss: Volume 2 – Separation, Anxiety and Anger,* Hogarth Press, London.

**Bowlby J,** 1978, *Attachment and Loss: Volume 3 – Loss, Sadness and Depression,* Penguin, Harmondsworth.

**Bowlby J,** 1988, *A Secure Base – Clinical Applications of Attachment Theory,* Routledge, London.

**Cardinal M,** 1993, *The Words to Say It: An Autobiographical Novel,* (Goodheart P, trans), Women's Press, London (originally published in French, 1975).

**Casement P,** 1985, *On Learning From the Patient,* Routledge, London.

**Casement P,** 1990, *Further Learning From the Patient: The Analytic Space and Process,* Tavistock/Routledge, London.

**Cook D**, 1991, *Second Best,* Faber & Faber, London.

**Fairbairn WRD,** 1952, 'Endopsychic Structure Considered in Terms of Object-Relationships', in *Psychoanalytic Studies of the Personality,* Tavistock/Routledge, London.

**Giovacchini PL,** 1989, *Countertransference Triumphs and Catastrophes,* Jason Aronson, Northvale, NJ.

**Helmlinger T,** 1982, *After You've Said Goodbye: Learning How to Stand Alone,* Brooks, Bakersfied, CA.

**Holme J,** 1996, *Attachment, Intimacy, Autonomy – Using Attachment Theory in Adult Psychotherapy,* Jason Aronson, New York.

**Hughes T,** 1995, *New Selected Poems 1957–1994,* Faber & Faber, London.

**Jackson J,** 1992, 'Screaming From Birth: Therapeutic Explorations of a Two Year Old's Failure to Find a Maternal Lap', *Journal of Child Psychology,* (18) 2.

**Kaplan L,** 1978, *Oneness and Separateness: From Infant to Individual,* Touchstone, New York.

**Kohut H,** 1984, *How Does Analysis Cure?,* University of Chicago, London/Chicago.

**Mahler M,** 1968, *On Human Symbiosis and the Vicissitudes of Individuation,* International Universities Press, New York.

**Montagu A,** 1971, *Touching: The Human Significance of the Skin,* Harper & Row, London.

**Murray L,** 1988, 'Effects of Postnatal Depression on Infant Development: Direct Studies of Early Mother Infant Reactions', in Kumar R & Brockington IF (eds), *Motherhood and Mental Illness 2: Causes and Consequences,* Wright, London/Boston.

**Odier C,** 1956, *Anxiety and Magical Thinking,* International Universities Press, New York.

**Okri B,** 1991, *The Famished Road,* Cape, London.

**Polster E & Polster M,** 1973, *Gestalt Therapy Integrated,* Brunner/Mazel, New York.

**Reid S,** 1990, 'The Importance of Beauty in the Psychoanalytic Experience', *Journal of Child Psychotherapy,* 16(1): 29–52.

**Robertson J & Robertson J,** 1969, 'John – 17 Months: Nine Days in a Residential Nursery', 16mm film/video, The Robertson Centre; accompanied by a printed 'Guide to the Film' series, British Medical Association/Concord Film Council.

**Schore A,** 1994, *Affect Regulation and the Origins of the Self. The Neurobiology of Emotional Development,* Lawrence Erlbaum Associates, New Jersey.

**Spitz R,** 1941, 'On Hospitalization', *Psychoanalytic Study of the Child,* 1: 3-74.

**Stern DN,** 1990, *Diary of a Baby – What Your Child Sees, Feels, and Experiences,* Basic Books, New York.

**Stern DN,** 1993, 'Acting versus Remembering in Transference Love and Infantile Love', in Spector-Person E, Hagelin A and Fonagy P (eds), *On Freud's 'Observations on Transference-Love',* Yale University Press, New Haven/London.

**Stewart I & Joines V,** 1987, *T A Today,* Lifespace, Nottingham.

**Sunderland M,** 1993, *Draw On Your Emotions,* Speechmark Publishing, Bicester.

**Sunderland M,** 2000, *Using Story Telling as a Therapeutic Tool with Children,* Speechmark Publishing, Bicester.

**Trevarthen C,** 1986, 'The self born in intersubjectivity: The psychology of an infant communicating', reprinted in Neisser U (ed), 1993, *The Perceived Self: Ecological and Interpersonal Sources of Self Knowledge,* Cambridge University Press, Cambridge/New York.

**Wilde O,** 1989, *The Sayings of Oscar Wilde,* Russell H, (ed), Duckworth, London.

**Woodman M,** 1985, *The Pregnant Virgin: A Process of Psychological Transformation,* Inner City Books, Toronto.